Does God Exist?

Crucial Questions booklets provide a quick introduction to definitive Christian truths. This expanding collection includes titles such as:

Who Is Jesus?

Can I Trust the Bible?

Does Prayer Change Things?

Can I Know God's Will?

How Should I Live in This World?

What Does It Mean to Be Born Again?

Can I Be Sure I'm Saved?

What Is Faith?

What Can I Do with My Guilt?

What Is the Trinity?

TO BROWSE THE REST OF THE SERIES, PLEASE VISIT: **REFORMATIONTRUST.COM/CQ**

CQ

Does God Exist?

R.C. SPROUL

R *Reformation Trust*   A DIVISION OF LIGONIER MINISTRIES, ORLANDO, FL

Does God Exist?
© 2019 by R.C. Sproul

Published by Reformation Trust Publishing
A division of Ligonier Ministries
421 Ligonier Court, Sanford, FL 32771
Ligonier.org   ReformationTrust.com

Printed in China
RR Donnelley
0001018
First edition

ISBN 978-1-64289-120-1 (Paperback)
ISBN 978-1-64289-121-8 (ePub)
ISBN 978-1-64289-122-5 (Kindle)

Cover design: Ligonier Creative
Interior typeset: Katherine Lloyd, The DESK

Scripture quotations are from the ESV® Bible (The Holy Bible, English Standard Version®), copyright © 2001 by Crossway, a publishing ministry of Good News Publishers. Used by permission. All rights reserved.

Library of Congress Cataloging-in-Publication Data

Names: Sproul, R.C. (Robert Charles), 1939-2017 author.
Title: Does God exist? / by R.C. Sproul.
Description: Orlando : Reformation Trust, 2019. | Series: Crucial Questions ; No. 29
Identifiers: LCCN 2018036546| ISBN 9781642891201 (Paperback) | ISBN 9781642891218 (ePub) | ISBN 9781642891225 (Kindle)
Subjects: LCSH: God--Proof.
Classification: LCC BT103 .S693 2019 | DDC 212/.1--dc23
LC record available at https://lccn.loc.gov/2018036546

Contents

Chapter One

The Case for God

Immanuel Kant's *Critique of Pure Reason* was a watershed moment in the history of theoretical thought. The book gives a comprehensive critique of the traditional arguments for the existence of God. It forced the church to wrestle with some important questions. How do we now approach apologetics (the defense of the faith)? How can we legitimately make a case for God without falling into the trap of the problems Kant posed? Several different approaches arose in response.

One view, known as fideism, maintained that we cannot convincingly argue for the existence of God. Instead, belief in God's existence must be based on faith. Many theologians and

Christians have adopted this viewpoint. Some even go so far as to say that people must simply take a leap of faith into the darkness and hope that someone out there will catch them.

There are flaws with this approach. Even though faith is central to biblical Christianity, there is a difference between faith and foolishness. Yet people often assert that the way of the Christian world is the way of faith to the exclusion of the way of reason. For example, the ancient church father Tertullian asked, "What does Jerusalem have to do with Athens?" He also said, "I believe Christianity because it is absurd." If by saying this Tertullian meant that Christianity is absurd from the world's perspective, that would be one thing. But if he meant that it's objectively absurd, that would be a serious slander against the character of God and the Holy Spirit, who is the Spirit of truth.

Another approach, called evidentialism, asserts that the way to defend the Christian faith is through appeals to history. Many apologists take this approach, acknowledging that while arguments from the field of history can never give absolute proof, they do offer a high degree of probability. That high degree of probability results in what is called moral certainty. While these arguments from biblical history may not give the same formal certainty that is found in logical deduction, they certainly are powerful enough that they leave people without any moral escape hatches.

In our American judicial system, when people are charged with serious crimes, the burden of proof rests on the prosecution. They must prove that the person is guilty beyond a reasonable doubt. Similarly, evidentialists attempt to show that the evidence of history so communicates and proves the existence of God that it is beyond a reasonable doubt. In fact, the evidence is so overwhelming that only a fool would deny their conclusion.

The problem with this approach is that even in the face of overwhelming probability, the sinner still has a tiny escape hatch to say: "You didn't prove it beyond a shadow of a doubt. Maybe it's not reasonable for me to doubt it, but you haven't proven your case conclusively." A philosopher named Gotthold Ephraim Lessing posed the metaphor of the great ditch that divides this world from the world of God. He said that the contingent things of events in history can never prove eternal things.

It is often thought that there are only two kinds of apologists—evidentialists (whom we have already discussed) and presuppositionalists (whom we will examine in a moment). Yet there is another school of thought called the classical school of apologetics. The difference between the classical school and the evidentialist school is this: evidentialists argue that the evidence drawn from history and elsewhere gives a high degree of probability for the existence of God, whereas classicists argue that proof for the existence of God is conclusive and compelling. It is actual proof that leaves people without any excuses whatsoever.

In contrast to evidentialism and classicism, the approach that has become the overwhelming majority view within Reformed theology is known as presuppositional apologetics. The most popular version was developed by Cornelius Van Til, who published much in this field and was a genuine titan of the Christian faith.

Van Til wrote in the English language but, since he was from the Netherlands and English was not his native tongue, he sometimes wrote in a style that is difficult to follow. Consequently, not only do his critics differ among themselves as to what he actually said, but some of his most noteworthy students differ in how they interpret him.

The presuppositional view says this: In order to arrive at the conclusion that God exists and to prove His existence, one must start with the primary premise of the existence of God. In other words, unless the existence of God is presupposed, one can never reach the conclusion that He exists. The objection immediately arises that this procedure involves the classic logical fallacy called *petitio principii*, the fallacy of circular reasoning, in which the conclusion appears in the premises. This is the chief objection raised against presuppositional apologetics.

Van Til, aware that such a charge would be made, defended against it by saying that all reasoning moves in a circular fashion, insofar as its starting point, middle ground, and conclusions are all involved with one another. If one starts with a rational premise and reasons consistently in a rational way, his conclusion will be of a rational sort. And so, with that definition, Van Til justified his use of circular reasoning, arguing that it was no different from any of the other approaches, because all reasoning is circular in that sense. However, this justification for circular reasoning contains two deadly fallacies.

The first fallacy is the fallacy of circular reasoning, which in classic categories of logic invalidates an argument. The justification for using circular reasoning introduces the second fallacy, the fallacy of equivocation, in which a term changes its meaning in the middle of the argument. Van Til justified circular reasoning by saying that all reasoning is circular (in the sense that its starting point and conclusion are of a similar sort), but that is not what is meant by the term *circular reasoning*. A rational argument, if it is to be rational, must be consistently rational throughout. Why call that a circle when in fact it is linear?

Granted, presuppositions are involved in rational argumentation: the presupposition of reason, the presupposition of the law of noncontradiction, the presupposition of causality, the presupposition of the basic reliability of sense perception, and the presupposition of the analogical use of language. Those who defend Van Til argue that he was getting at something deeper than a superficial exercise in circular reasoning. Instead, they claim, he was saying that even assuming rationality necessarily involves presupposing the existence of God, because without God, there is no foundation for rational argumentation. So, even though a person may not want to admit it, advocating for reason assumes the ground of that reason, which is God Himself.

Classicists certainly agree that if rationality is to be meaningful, and if the presuppositions of epistemology are sound, then they scream for the existence of God. But that is exactly what classical apologetics is trying to prove. We must show people that if they want to be rational, they must affirm the existence of God, because the very rationality that they presuppose demands the existence of God.

The biggest objection to presuppositionalism, beside these logical errors, is that no one starts with God except God. One cannot start in his mind with God and the knowledge of God unless he is God. Human beings start with self-consciousness and then move from there to the existence of God. They do not start with God-consciousness and move to the existence of the self. By necessity, human beings thinking with human minds must start where they are.

The theologian Augustine of Hippo said that with self-consciousness always immediately comes an awareness of finitude—the moment that we are aware of ourselves as selves, we know that we are not God. The idea of autonomy, in which a person is a law unto himself, is not contained in the idea of self-consciousness. If it were, it would indeed be sinful to start at that point. But what we are actually saying is this: beginning with self-consciousness is a given to creatureliness. It's the only place any of us can start in our thinking. We cannot start with the thoughts of others or the thoughts of God. The only place we can start is our own self-awareness, and from there we move on and soon discover that we are not autonomous at all.

If we begin with self-consciousness and reason correctly, far from ending in autonomy, we will by necessity end up affirming the existence of God. The fear among presuppositionalists is that in arguing rationally and empirically, they give too much away to the pagan world. And the fear of the classicists toward the presuppositionalists is precisely the same thing: they give too much away. They give the pagan an excuse for not believing in the existence of God because the pagan can see that their approach violates principles of rationality.

Yet, regardless of the differing views on apologetics within Reformed theology, we all agree that the reality of the existence of God is the single most important premise in the building of one's life and worldview. We know that according to Romans 1, the first lie that the pagan embraces is the denial of the eternal power and deity of God. As a result, his mind becomes darkened, and the more brilliant he is, the further away he moves from that first awareness of God that he receives in nature.

Therefore, we all agree in the supreme importance of establishing early on in our apologetics the existence of God. In the next chapter, we'll begin to demonstrate how classical apologetics constructs its case for the existence of God.

Chapter Two

Four Possibilities

The classical method of apologetics is modeled after another method that in its rudimentary form was established by Augustine of Hippo many centuries ago. His approach sought to establish a sufficient reason that would explain reality as we encounter it. Augustine also approached this question by looking at it via a process of elimination: he examined possible theoretical options and then tested them to see whether they passed the test of rationality.

We start with four basic possibilities for explaining reality as we encounter it. The first is that our experience of reality is itself an illusion. The second is that reality as we encounter it is self-created. The third possibility is that the reality we encounter is self-existent. And the fourth possibility is that reality is created ultimately by something else that is self-existent.

For example, consider this book. According to the four major possibilities for explaining reality, either (1) the book is an illusion and is not really there, (2) the book has ultimately created itself, (3) the book is self-existent, or (4) the book ultimately came into being as the result of something else that is self-existent. To give a sufficient reason for the existence of the book, one of these four possibilities must be true. Further, if one of them is true, the others must be false.

The vast majority of atheists who want to account for the world as we know it fall back on some concept of self-creation, such as the Big Bang theory (option 2), while the minority argue that the universe is itself self-existent and eternal (option 3). But for the most part, even those who argue for a self-existent universe at least agree that there is a self-existent *something*. The question is, What is it? Is that something a spiritual, transcendent, immaterial something called God, or is it matter itself? Reason demands the existence of a self-existent, eternal something in order to account for the existence of anything in this world, and therefore one cannot be consistently rational by denying the necessity of a self-existent, eternal something. Both reason and science demand the existence of a self-existent, eternal something to account for the existence of anything else.

The difference between the classical approach to apologetics and the evidential approach is that the evidentialist tries to give an argument from probability based upon physical or empirical evidence, that is, evidence that is available to the five senses. However, there is a built-in limitation to the value of empirical evidence: it never delivers what is called formal or absolute rational proof, proof that carries the force of logical compulsion, such as can be found in mathematics (e.g., two plus two equals four).

The classical approach seeks to give compelling proof of the existence of this self-existent, eternal something that goes beyond the level of mere probability (and therefore differs from the evidentialist approach). There is a difference between giving good evidence and giving absolute proof. The classicist seeks to show people not just evidence but proof. In order for that to be the case, we can't start with a book, because if we assume the existence of the book, we are simultaneously assuming sense perception and the physical reality of the book, which immediately throws us into the arena of the empirical and the sensational, that is, what I perceive with the senses, which can never get me to absolute philosophical proof.

A rational proof compels a rational person to acquiesce to its conclusions. John Calvin popularized the notion of distinguishing between proof and persuasion. The difference is that proof is objective, while persuasion is subjective. Based on the premises that all men are mortal and Socrates is a man, I can conclude beyond a shadow of a doubt that Socrates is mortal. That is a logically compelling conclusion, given the premises.

However, someone could offer a proof that is logically conclusive, compelling, and rationally certain, and people could simply refuse to accept it. We have all met people who, despite all reason and evidence, refuse to acquiesce to the truth because of emotional reasons or biases.

This is what John Calvin sought to convey in the beginning of his *Institutes of the Christian Religion* when he discussed Scripture. He believed that Scripture gives objective evidence to stop the mouths of even the most stubborn—that it is, in fact, the Word of God, and the indications and evidences for its supernatural origin are clear. However, Calvin also argued that because man is so ill-disposed toward the things of God and has such a profound bias against the truth of God, he will never be sufficiently convinced until or unless God the Holy Spirit changes the disposition of his heart. The true problem when it comes to man's view of Scripture, Calvin says, is not an intellectual one so much as it is a moral one.

That is exactly what we encounter when we engage with the question of the existence of God. There is an enormous amount at stake, because if we can prove without a doubt that the eternal God of the universe exists, then that means that all people will be held accountable for how they live. Therefore, one reason that people want to get rid of the idea of God is to be free from guilt and accountability. The unbeliever strongly desires the evidence for God not to be compelling.

Even if our argument is as compelling as God's own argument, that doesn't mean that everyone will be willing to admit to it. But it is not our task to convince anyone that God exists. We are not called to convince people, but we *are* called to give a reason for the hope that is within us, and we are called to be faithful to that responsibility.

Chapter Three

The Illusion of Descartes

To many people, it might seem like a huge waste of time to try to eliminate the first of the four possibilities for explaining reality—that everything we think exists is an illusion. However, the pages of history include serious philosophers who have argued precisely that point: that the world and everything in it is simply someone else's dream, or it is basically illusory and doesn't exist at all. To address this first possibility, we turn to René Descartes. Descartes was a seventeenth-century philosopher, mathematician, and the father of modern rationalism. He was concerned about a new form of skepticism that had arrived in Western Europe after the sixteenth-century Protestant Reformation.

Before the Reformation, Christians who had disputes with one another could appeal to the authority of the Roman Catholic Church to render a verdict. When the verdict was handed down, that settled the controversy, because the authority of the church was deemed to be at least inviolable and possibly infallible. With the challenge to the authority of the church that came with the Protestant Reformation, the question "How can we know anything for sure?" became a serious problem.

The breakdown of church authority was accompanied by a breakdown of scientific authority. The sixteenth century witnessed the Copernican revolution in astronomy, which created an enormous crisis in the tradition of scientific authority that had followed the ancient Ptolemaic system of the universe. Copernicus turned that system on its head, raising all kinds of questions about the trustworthiness of science. This controversy over the Copernican revolution carried over into the seventeenth century, where the Galileo episode became prominent in the life of the church. Galileo pointed his telescope toward the heavens and confirmed the mathematical theories of sixteenth-century astronomers.

Descartes sought to reestablish some foundation for certainty with respect to truth. He was looking for what he called "clear and distinct ideas"—ideas that were indubitable, ideas that could not be rejected without at the same time rejecting reason. These ideas could then form a foundation for the reconstruction of knowledge, whether in science or in theology and philosophy.

The process Descartes followed in order to achieve certainty followed the path of uncertainty. He embarked on a rigorous pursuit of skepticism in order to bring doubt on everything he could conceivably doubt. In other words, he wanted to give a second glance to every assumed truth that people held, asking the epistemological question, Do we really know that this is true?

We too must subject our own thinking to rigorous cross-examination; we must examine our ideas to make sure they're true. However, this does not mean that we must surrender to skepticism as Descartes did. His approach was to doubt everything he could conceivably doubt—even what he saw with his eyes and heard with his ears, for he reasoned that his senses could be deceived. Further, Descartes thought that perhaps the world was controlled by a great deceiver—a master of illusion who constantly gives people a false view of reality. How, then, can we know that reality is as we perceive it to be?

We must start with basic principles in order to arrive at knowledge, including the basic reliability of sense perception. For if we cannot trust our senses, then we have no way of getting outside the interior of our minds and making contact with an external world. This is known as the subject-object problem. In other words, how do we know that the objective world out there is as we perceive it from within our own perspective?

Descartes was acutely aware of this problem. He concluded that it is impossible to escape the reality of doubt. He raised this question: What is required for there to be doubt? He believed that doubt requires cognition, because doubt is an act of thinking. Without thinking, there can be no doubting. So if someone is doubting, that means he is thinking. Then he went to the next premise that just as doubt requires a doubter, thought requires a thinker. So if he was doubting, he had to rationally conclude that he was thinking, and if he was thinking, he must exist, or be. He must exist because that which does not exist cannot think, and that which cannot think cannot doubt, and since there was no doubt that he was doubting, it would mean also that he was thinking, and if was thinking, he was also existing. After he went through this elaborate doubting process, he came to the famous motto for which he is so well known: *Cogito ergo sum*—"I think, therefore, I am."

People who are not students of philosophy look at Descartes' elaborate process and conclude that philosophy is foolish. How could someone spend so much time and effort to learn what everyone already knows—that they do in fact exist? No one really denies his own existence. People don't believe that they are simply a star appearing in someone else's dream. However, remember who Descartes was. He was a mathematician looking for certainty in the philosophical realm that would equal in force, power, and rational compulsion the certainty that can be arrived at in mathematics.

Descartes was getting at the concept that whatever else may be in doubt, the fact that he was a self-conscious existing person was not in doubt. He did not have to look at his own feet to know that he existed. He was not dependent on any external perception or data, for he learned it simply from the interior processes of thought in his mind.

He stayed within the realm of rational deduction for his conclusion.

Through this process, Descartes disposed of the first of the four options regarding reality: that it is an illusion. There may indeed be illusions in reality, but if we say that *all* reality is an illusion, that would mean that nothing exists, including the self, and one cannot doubt the existence of the self without proving the reality of the self. Descartes demonstrated that the idea of reality as illusion is not a sufficient explanation for reality and must be discarded, for his argument proved that something does indeed exist.

Descartes made two important major assumptions in order to arrive at his conclusion. The first assumption is that because he was doubting, he must have been thinking. This involves an epistemological principle known as the law of noncontradiction, which states that it is not possible for something to be and not be at the same time and in the same relation. Descartes said he could not *be* a doubter and *not be* a doubter at the same time and in the same relation. This is a logical conclusion based on the law of noncontradiction.

The second of Descartes' assumptions was that if he was thinking, he must have been existing. This assumption involves the law of causality, which states that every effect has an antecedent cause. When he said that doubting requires a doubter, he was saying that doubt is an effect that requires a cause. Critics of Descartes might say that this doesn't prove that he exists, because he's assuming logic and causality, which they might not accept. Again, this is irrational, because the law of causality is simply an extension of the law of noncontradiction. Something cannot *be* an effect and *not be* an effect (i.e., by not having a cause) at the same time in the same relation. The law of causality is a formal truth. It's as formally true as two plus two equals four, because it's true by definition.

We dare not negotiate the law of noncontradiction and the law of causality, because if we do, we'll end up in absurdity. These principles are necessary for all intelligible discourse in science, philosophy, and theology. If we use them, then we cannot escape Descartes' conclusion that we can—through a resistless logic and through formal reasoning alone—conclude the fact of our own existence, which then invalidates the idea that all reality is an illusion. Therefore, we can eliminate the idea that illusion explains the perception of the existence of the world.

Chapter Four

Self-Creation, Part 1

In the previous chapter, we eliminated the first of four possible alternatives to account for reality: that everything is an illusion. We now come to the second option: self-creation. Self-creation is the most frequent alternative that atheists present to theism, which is belief in some sort of god or gods. It's rare that someone will come right out and say that the universe is self-created. However, though people may not articulate their view under the name of self-creation, their belief can be subsumed under that category.

Before examining some variations on the theme of self-creation, it must be acknowledged that the idea of self-creation is a concept that, according to philosophy, is analytically false. That is, it is false by definition. Self-creation is manifestly absurd, because for something to create itself, to be its own creator and to be an effect that is its own cause, it would have to exist before it existed.

To put it another way, in order to create itself, it would have to be before it was. That would mean that something would have to be and not be at the same time in the same relationship, which violates the law of noncontradiction and places this idea in the realm of irrationality and absurdity. For something to create itself, it would have to antedate itself. It would have to be before it was. So the idea of self-creation is, by logical analysis, a false premise.

Even so, different theories of self-creation have been articulated throughout history. One of the most widespread attempts took place during the Enlightenment, and it was an attempt to avoid the idea of a self-existent creator God. In the French encyclopedic movement, people such as Denis Diderot and Baron d'Holbach argued vociferously against the existence of God. For them, the chief principle of the Enlightenment was the idea that now, with the advent of modern science in the eighteenth century, the God hypothesis was no longer necessary to explain, account for, or provide a sufficient cause for the universe. The encyclopedists argued that the God hypothesis could be rejected with impunity, for they believed that the material things in the universe came into being through spontaneous generation.

Spontaneous generation means that things simply begin on their own, suddenly and without any developmental period. People of that day would go outside and see mud puddles in the street that had developed overnight. They would look at the mud puddles and, seeing tiny fish eggs or tadpoles, would conclude that life was spontaneously coming out of the mud puddle. They didn't understand that those eggs or tadpoles got there somehow, such as being dropped by birds. The causes for the origin of those fish eggs or tadpoles were not apparent to them, so they concluded that there were no causes. So, there was a period of time in history where people believed that things appeared *ex nihilo*, "out of nothing."

A fundamental premise of science is *ex nihilo nihil fit*: "out of nothing, nothing comes." Nothing does not produce something because nothing cannot produce something.

However, this principle was challenged in the Enlightenment with the concept of spontaneous generation.

The idea of spontaneous generation, though sometimes ridiculed today, is still around. Now, some say that we can affirm "gradual spontaneous generation," a process by which you can get something from nothing, but it takes time. You have to wait for this nothing to yield something. It may take eons and eons, but if you have enough patience, sooner or later, nothing can create something.

This is the point at which the philosopher and the scientist butt heads. In affirming spontaneous generation of any kind, the scientist has left behind rationality. When we analyze these concepts of spontaneous generation, what we find is a sophisticated attempt to articulate this idea of self-creation.

When the Hubble telescope was launched, a prominent astrophysicist spoke about the significance of "now increasing our understanding of outer space and changing the horizons by virtue of this new technology." He went on to explain how the beginning of the universe took place fifteen to eighteen billion years ago "when the universe exploded into being."

The astrophysicist used language that is heavily conditioned by philosophy: the word "being" is filled with philosophical content. Further, he didn't say the universe exploded into its present form. It's one thing to say that before a point fifteen to eighteen billion years ago, the universe was in one form—that it existed, it was real, there was substance, it had being—and then it changed dramatically with the Big Bang. But this physicist used the phrase "exploded into being." What did he mean? What was it before the explosion? Was it the opposite of being, the antithesis of being, which in philosophical categories is nonbeing—a synonym for nothing?

So according to various advocates of self-creation, it takes not only a significant amount of time, but also an enormous explosion, for something to come out of nothing. And if we go back far enough in time—eighteen billion years perhaps—we can purportedly find this great explosion where reality came into being from nonreality. That is philosophical nonsense and sheer irrationality.

Yet this concept of gradual spontaneous generation, in which the universe exploded into being, is the most frequent form of self-creation that we meet in the modern culture. It is the idea of creation by chance—namely, that the universe came into being through some power attributed to chance, and the formula typically used is space plus time plus chance.

The oldest question in philosophy and science is, Why is there something rather than nothing? If there was ever a time when there was nothing—no God, no matter, no anything—what could there possibly be now? If there were ever a time when there was absolutely nothing, the only way to explain the presence of something would be through some kind of self-creator, something coming out of nothing by itself. However, self-creation is absolutely impossible.

Chapter Five

Self-Creation, Part 2

The most popular alternative to theism today consists of an appeal to "chance creation." The author Arthur Koestler astutely noted, "As long as chance rules, God is an anachronism." To take Koestler's remark a bit further, it's not even necessary for chance to rule—all that must be demonstrated to make God an anachronism is that chance simply *exists*.

The mere existence of chance is enough to rip God from His cosmic throne. Even if it exists as a mere impotent humble servant, it still leaves God not only out of date but out of a job. But the truth is, there is no such thing as chance—even though the greatest myth in modern society today is the myth of chance.

Of course, there is nothing inherently wrong with using the word *chance*. It is perfectly meaningful when we use it to describe mathematical possibilities. In that sense, it serves as a synonym for *odds*. We can ask, "What are the odds that something will happen?" or we can ask, "What are the chances that something will happen?" On the level of everyday conversation, we also make meaningful use of the term *chance* when we speak of "chance encounters," in which events occur that we did not intentionally plan, design, or intend.

However, chance does not explain *why* such instances occur. For example, years ago, while on a train ride from Orlando to Los Angeles, I had an eight-hour layover in Chicago. Walking through the station, which was crowded with a teeming mass of humanity because it was the morning commuter rush hour, I ran into a friend I hadn't seen in ten years. And eight hours later, as I was boarding the train for Los Angeles during evening rush hour, I ran into him yet *again*.

Though we might refer to this as a chance encounter, chance did not *cause* this event. The reason we met each other is that we happened to be at the same place at the same time for a host of different reasons that converged in time and space. However, *chance* is a perfectly legitimate word to use when we use it in a popular way to describe these types of unintentional meetings or to discuss mathematical probabilities.

However, what has happened in modern jargon is that the word *chance* has subtly been elevated to indicate something far more than mathematical odds or probabilities: actual *causal power* is attributed to chance. The ontological status of chance is zero (*ontology* referring to the study of being, essence, and reality). Chance has no being. Chance is not a thing that operates and works upon other things. It is simply a mental concept that refers to mathematical possibilities, but in and of itself, it has no being.

Let's return to our illustration of this book as an example. The book has some kind of being, and for centuries, physicists and philosophers have been busily engaged trying to penetrate the ultimate form of essence or substance that is found in a book (or any other thing that exists). What all will agree upon is that this book is not nothing—it is something. It has ontological status. It exists. It is not an illusion but real.

By contrast, chance has no being. And because it has no being, it therefore has no power, because that which is absent of being must of necessity also be absent of power. Power cannot be generated by nothing any more than objects can be generated by nothing. Power, or doing, requires a doer, just as René Descartes noted that thought requires a thinker.

Regarding the concept of chance, philosophers and scientists agree that the word is used to define our ignorance. People throw the word *chance* into the equation when they cannot explain something or reach a cogent understanding. So, they refer to "the power of chance." But since chance is not a thing that can exercise power, and in fact, has no existence at all, when people say that the universe was created by chance, they are actually saying that the universe was created by nothing. In doing so, they not only attribute some power to chance, but they attribute to it the most supreme power that can possibly be conceived of. They declare that not only can chance do something, but that it can bring into being the whole of reality.

Such a belief soon yields its own absurdity and manifests itself as the worst kind of mythology. No matter how much it may be couched in the language of science, and no matter how much respectability it may garner when these myths are dressed in academic terminology, the fact is that when people start attributing any power to chance, they have started speaking nonsense, because chance is nothing.

It is appropriate for a scientist to say he doesn't know why something is happening, that current scientific paradigms cannot explain, say, the behavior of subatomic particles. At that point, he is exercising a proper demeanor for scientific investigation. When he bumps into the limits of his knowledge, he says, "I don't know." This is what should be done in biology, chemistry, physics, philosophy, and theology. That should be the mark of any authentic investigator of truth.

However, it's quite another thing to say, "Nothing is producing this effect," because in order to know that, one would have to know every conceivable possible force that exists in or outside the universe, and the only way to have that kind of knowledge is to be omniscient. As a matter of prudence, we must stop saying that nothing causes something. It is a nonsense statement and pure mythology. It is not only bad theology but also bad science to espouse the concept of self-creation under any name.

Chapter Six

Self-Existence

We have been looking at the four options to explain reality as we now encounter it. The first option—that everything is an illusion—was eliminated, borrowing heavily from the arguments of René Descartes. The second option—that reality is self-created—was exposed as absurd by definition since it is rationally and logically impossible. The remaining options both involve the concept of self-existence. The third says that the universe itself is self-existent, and the fourth argues that the universe is not self-existent but was created by something that *is* self-existent. Since the first two options are impossible, clearly *something* must be self-existent in order for the universe around us to exist.

But before delving into what that self-existent something is, it is necessary to address the question of whether it is possible for anything to be self-existent. We have already seen that it is logically impossible for something to be self-created, because to create itself, it would have to exist before it existed, and it would therefore have to be and not be at the same time in the same relationship. Logic eliminates this as a rational possibility.

But is it a rational possibility for something to be self-existent and eternal? We've denied self-creation on the grounds that it is rationally impossible, but when we put these two concepts side by side—self-creation and self-existence—they seem so similar. If self-creation is rationally impossible, then must self-existence also be rationally impossible?

Here is the difference: there is nothing illogical in the idea of something that is self-existent and eternal—that is, something that was not caused by something else. One of the problems we encounter in the discussion of the existence of God is that some people misunderstand the law of cause and effect by thinking that it means *everything* must have a cause. But the law of causality simply says that every effect must have a cause, because an effect, by definition, is that which has been produced by something outside of or beyond itself. Therefore, the idea of an uncaused something is perfectly rational. Reason allows for this possibility, whereas it does not allow for the possibility of self-creation. We can safely conceive of the idea of a self-existent, eternal something without violating rationality.

In theology, the concept of self-existence is referred to as the attribute of *aseity*. This means that something exists in and of itself. It is uncaused, uncreated, and differs from everything in the universe that is dependent, derived, contingent, and has a cause. And so, this idea of a self-existent, eternal something that has aseity means that it possesses the power of being in and of itself.

Such a thing doesn't gain its existence or its being from something antecedent to itself; it possesses it inherently. And because it possesses it inherently, it also possesses it eternally. There was never a time that a self-existent thing did not exist. If it did, then it would be not self-existent— it would have to have been created by something else. And so a self-existent thing is, by definition, one that always has been.

Because something exists now, and because that something could not have created itself, that means there could never have been a time when there was absolutely nothing. There has always had to be something. So far, we have not yet demonstrated that this something is God. We are only arguing at this point that there must be *something* that has the power of being within itself and that has always existed. Given the thesis that something exists now (as opposed to nothing existing now), our next step must be to demonstrate that that something is by rational necessity a self-existent *being*. When we talk about God as a necessary being, we mean that His existence is a necessity of rational postulation; that is, reason demands the existence of a self-existent, eternal being.

And that is very important for Christians trying to defend their faith, because criticism of Judeo-Christianity is aimed almost exclusively at the ideas of creation and a Creator. After all, if people can get rid of creation and a Creator, then the whole concept of God collapses. It is argued that in order to be scientific and rational, one must believe in a universe without God. What Christians must do is seek to show these people that in reality, they need to turn their criticism on themselves, for what they postulate as an alternative to the idea of a self-existent Creator is utter irrationality and absurdity. Reason demands that there be a necessary being.

However, defining a necessary being in terms of rational necessity is not the only way to define necessary being. The other way to define it, as Thomas Aquinas did, is to say that this being has what is called "ontological necessity." This concept is a bit more abstract and slightly more difficult to understand. *Ontology* is the study or the science of being. When we say that God is ontologically necessary, we mean that He exists by the necessity of His own being. He exists not because reason says He has to exist; He exists eternally because He has the power of being in Himself, in such a way that He cannot *not* be.

That is the difference between us and God. We say that God is the supreme being and we are human beings, but the difference between the supreme being and the human being is that our being, our existence, is a creaturely existence in which we are dependent, derived, and contingent. To exist in our present state, we need water, oxygen, and a host of other necessities to sustain us, and we are dependent on all of these things to continue to exist. Not only that, the whole process or progress of our lives is a constant cycle of generation and decay, a continual change. Change is the supreme characteristic of contingent beings.

Further, our lives can be measured in terms of time. A hundred years ago, none of us existed. There was a time when we were not, and there will come a time in the future when the form in which we now live will undergo a transition. We cannot sustain ourselves forever; we will all die.

Creatures change constantly, whereas that which has self-existent, eternal being is changeless. It will never lose any power of its being, nor does it gain anything in the scope of its being, because it is what it is eternally. It has being itself within its own power. That is what we mean by a self-existent, eternal something whose being is ontologically necessary. It cannot help but be. Pure being is dependent on nothing for its continuity of existence or its origin of existence. It is not in a state of becoming; it is in a state of pure being, and pure being cannot *not* be.

This is precisely how God revealed Himself with His sacred name to Moses in the Midianite wilderness. God called to Moses out of the burning bush and sent him on a mission to Pharaoh to liberate the people of Israel. Moses, in amazement, watched a bush that was burning but not being consumed, and he heard a voice speaking to him out of the bush: "When the LORD saw that he turned aside to see, God called to him out of the bush, "Moses, Moses! . . . Do not come near; take your sandals off your feet, for the place on which you are standing is holy ground. . . . I am the God of your father, the God of Abraham, the God of Isaac, and the God of Jacob" (Ex. 3:4–6). When Moses asked God what to say when people asked him God's name, He said, "I AM WHO I AM. . . . Say this to the people of Israel: 'I AM has sent me to you'" (v. 14).

God answered Moses by giving him His sacred name, His memorial name, the name by which He is known from all generations: Yahweh, which means, "I am who I am." "I am" was sending Moses, not "I was" or "I will be" or "I'm in the process of change or becoming," but "I am who I am." God uses the verb "to be" in the present tense. This is the name of God, the One whose being is eternally present and eternally unchanging, without whose being nothing else could possibly be.

Because something now exists, reason demands that something or someone be self-existent. But is this self-existent, eternal being God, or is it the universe itself? We will explore this question in the next chapter.

Chapter Seven

Necessary Being

The various theories advanced to explain the origins of the universe change—and sometimes undergo revolutionary upheavals—from time to time. The advent of the Big Bang theory of the origin of the universe, which was not accepted at all in the middle of the twentieth century, is almost universally accepted today within the scientific community.

The Big Bang is usually described as a time in past history where all that existed at the time, usually described as a point of singularity (i.e., a point of infinite smallness and infinite density) was a compaction of all matter and energy in the universe. At some point—now thought to be 13.8

billion years ago—this point of singularity exploded (for reasons unknown to us) and out of that explosion came the matter and energy that we observe in the material universe as we know it today.

The Big Bang theory purports that at one time, whatever existed was in a state of high organization, in that it was in a stable form (i.e., it was not then exploding) in a single location. The second law of thermodynamics indicates that everything is increasing in entropy or disorganization. But if the state of nature is to inherently move toward disorganization, then how did it become organized in the first place?

The other law that must first be addressed is the law of inertia, which states that objects in motion tend to remain in motion unless acted upon by an outside force, and objects at rest tend to remain at rest unless acted upon by an outside force. For example, imagine a golfer with a golf ball. When the ball is placed on the tee, it is at rest. It will stay there unless and until it is acted upon by an outside force, such as when the golfer strikes it with his club. It will then remain in motion unless and until it is acted upon by an outside force—air resistance slows it down, until it eventually lands, whereupon it experiences friction from the ground and rolls to a stop.

If things at rest tend to stay at rest and things in motion tend to stay in motion, then the biggest question about the Big Bang is this: What caused the bang? Many people have argued that answering this question is unnecessary—that it goes beyond science and into the arena of philosophy, theology, or religion. Yet if this theory is being offered as an explanation for all of reality, and all of one's hopes are pinned on the concept of a Big Bang, then how can one not answer the question?

Scientific theory is innately concerned with matters of causality, and this is the big question of causality: What caused the Big Bang? It is nothing but an academic and intellectual cop-out to evade the question or consider it unnecessary to answer. Anyone who chooses to offer this thesis for the origin of everything must reckon with the question of what outside force caused this monumental change in a little point of singularity.

The answer to that question is readily available in biblical Christianity. The doctrine of creation teaches that there is a self-existent, eternal being who possesses the power of motion and has the ability to move that which is not moving. The philosopher Aristotle understood this; he spoke of the need for an "unmoved mover." He knew that there must be an origin to motion, and that which has the origin of motion must have the power of motion within itself, just as it must have the power of being within itself. That is why we attribute these qualities to God.

There is still, however, the idea that the matter and energy compacted in the Big Bang point of singularity are self-existent and eternal. The assertion, then, is that the universe is not 13.8 billion years old; only the present motion of the universe goes back to that point. But the actual ingredients or stuff of reality is eternal. This view is called materialism.

Yet how do we determine which things in the universe are eternal? Is this book in its individuated form eternal? What about a set of car keys? Of course, the materialist will answer that those things are manufactured. After all, the materialist knows that the chief characteristic of matter is its mutability—it changes from one state into another state and is not stable eternally. That is how we are able to make things into other things.

But this is what the materialist will then say: "We grant that this book is not the eternal reality that is self-existent. Rather, it is made up of elements that are generated by a self-existent, eternal something. But this self-existent, eternal something—contrary to what Christians believe—is not transcendent, but immanent." That is, the materialist argues that we do not have to appeal to something above and beyond this universe to account for this universe. He argues against what Christianity, Judaism, and Islam all teach—that outside the whole realm of the creaturely universe stands a self-existent, eternal being whom we call God, who is the Creator of all things, and in Him all things live and move and have their being. So, we say that one of the chief characteristics of God is that He transcends the universe.

The materialist understands and agrees that something must be self-existent and eternal and have the power of being within itself. He would not retreat to the idea of self-creation and would grant its absurdity. However, he would not grant that this self-existent, eternal something is a God who is separate from and above the universe. Instead, he would consider God, if He exists, to be either part of the universe or the sum total of it. But the sum total of the universe would include this book. And if we say that God is the sum total of the universe, then we must include this book as part of God and therefore self-existent and eternal. Yet we know that the book is not self-existent and eternal because it can disintegrate. It can be torn in half. It can be reduced and changed.

It is at the point the materialist would agree that the book has an individuated, particular existence that is contingent, but he would then argue that underlying it is some universal material that underlies everything that is. And this material is self-existent and eternal and has power and being in itself. This material accounts for the explosion of the point of singularity 13.8 billion years ago. And everything else is generated through the power that comes from this material.

Note the use of the word *generate* here. The first book of the Old Testament is called Genesis, from the Greek word *gennaō*, which means "to be, to become, to happen." To make something come into existence is to generate it or cause it to be. So, the materialist conceives of some unknown point or material within the universe that is the source of all reality and that generates everything from the beginning. There is no God who lives outside the universe and is above and beyond the universe. Instead, this self-existent, eternal generating power is part of the universe itself.

This view is popular in certain circles in science and philosophy today. Yes, there is a self-existent, eternal power, without which there can be nothing. So far, those who hold to this view agree with those who affirm God's existence.

But there is a challenge issued to believers in God: Why do we say that the self-existent, eternal power must transcend the universe? Why can't it be a part of the universe itself? The answer is that it can be part of the universe, depending on how you define *universe*. If by the term *universe* we mean all that is, and if God is, then God would be subsumed under the term *universe*. If, however, the term *universe* is meant to refer to the created universe, then obviously we cannot subsume God into the meaning of *universe*.

However, we must distinguish between God and the universe, and the distinction that we make in theology is that God transcends the universe. It is critical to note that transcendence does not give a description of God's location. Transcendence is not a geographical description. We are not saying that God is transcendent in the sense that He lives somewhere out there, east of the sun and west of the moon. What is meant by transcendence in philosophy and theology is that something is a higher order of being. That is, transcendence is actually an ontological description, not a geographic one.

When we say that God is transcendent, we simply mean that He is a higher order of being than we are. He is a higher order of being than this book is. He is a higher order of being than the sun is. He is a higher order of being than pure energy is.

Those who argue that there is some unknown, invisible, immeasurable point or material within the universe that is self-existent and eternal and from which everything else is generated are ultimately agreeing with the Christian worldview. They affirm the existence of something that is above, prior to, and different from all the derivative, dependent, derived, contingent things that are generated by and from it. At that point, we are just arguing over its name. But regardless, we are forced back to a self-existent, eternal something from whose being and by whose power all things come into existence.

Many Christians object at this point. They grant that philosophy and reason argue for and demonstrate that we must have a self-existent, eternal something. But how do we get from that to the God of the Bible? So far, all we have is Aristotle's "unmoved mover" and an abstract idea of a self-existent, eternal something. We haven't come yet to the God of the Bible. Thus far, the argument has been based more on philosophy than on biblical exegesis. So the question remains: What is the relationship between the god of the philosophers and the God of the Bible?

Chapter Eight

The God of the Bible vs. the God of Philosophy

While the concept of a self-existent, eternal something has been established, we are still a long way from the personal being that we encounter in Judeo-Christianity—the God of the Bible. Some might argue that all we have established is a being akin to the god of the philosophers—an abstract concept of a self-existent, eternal being. That leaves us with two serious questions to address. The first is, What is the relationship between this philosophical concept and the God of the Bible? And the second is, How do we get from a self-existent, eternal being to a personal God?

The early church father Tertullian was famous for his credo "I believe because it's absurd." In saying this, Tertullian sought to illustrate the radical difference between the God of the Bible and the god of the Greek philosophers. When he asked, "What does Jerusalem have to do with Athens?" he meant it rhetorically, meaning there is no point of contact between the personal God of the Israelites and the vague, abstract concept or principle found in Greek philosophy.

Tertullian's objection resurfaced in the nineteenth century in the form of liberal theology. Figures such as church historian Adolf von Harnack and theologian Albrecht Ritschl said that early in its history, the church was corrupted by the intrusion of Greek philosophy. As early as the Council of Nicaea in the fourth century—which defined the Trinity by saying that God is one in essence and three in person—the categories and phrases the church used were laden with Greek philosophical concepts. The nineteenth-century liberals argued that the church must break free from the stranglehold that Greek philosophy had on the thinking of theologians through the ages.

This view of liberalism has made enormous inroads into the evangelical church of the twentieth and twenty-first centuries. As a result, many people in the church have begun to reject systematic theology, which seeks a rational, coherent understanding of the whole scope of Scripture. The charge is that systematicians impose a philosophical system on the Bible and try to squeeze everything to fit into this preconceived system that is borrowed from Greek philosophy.

But the task of systematic theology is never to impose a foreign system on the Scriptures and then force the Scriptures to fit into it. Rather, systematicians look at the whole scope of Scripture and seek to develop a coherent understanding by finding the system of thought that is in the Bible, not a system that we impose on it. This presupposes that when God speaks, He speaks coherently. It also presupposes that God has given us minds to understand His Word in a coherent, rational way. And yet this anti-systemic concept today is linked in many cases to the antipathy that people have toward Greek philosophy.

In light of this antipathy, we must remember that God the Holy Spirit chose Greek as the language in which the

New Testament would be written. As a result, the language of the Greeks is with us forever in terms of our understanding of the gospel. This does not mean that we should interpret New Testament Greek strictly in light of Greek philosophy. Even though the language is Greek, the concepts come from the Hebrew world. They were simply communicated through the Greek language.

What, though, is the difference between the idea of God that one finds in Aristotle and the idea of God that we find in Christianity? Aristotle defined God as "thought thinking itself," the "unmoved mover," and the "first cause of all things." But the god of Aristotle did not create through a voluntary act but rather out of necessity. He remained completely impersonal, remote, and removed from the world that he generated from his being.

According to Christianity, the God we find in the Bible is, on the first verse of the first page, introduced as the One who acted to create all that is, and who acted in a reasonable, purposeful manner to bring things to pass. And that which He created, He sustains and commits Himself to. That is the biblical view of creation and redemption: that God is intimately concerned with the affairs of history and with managing the universe that He created. There are obviously sharp differences in the view of God that we find in Aristotle and the view of God that we find in the Scriptures.

In Greek philosophy, the concept of the *logos*, or the "word," functions as an abstract idea that is necessary to give order and harmony to the world. But in biblical Christianity, the *logos* is the incarnate Word of God, a person, the Lord Jesus Christ. This is a massive departure from what we find regarding the *logos* in Stoicism or in the thinking of the philosopher Heraclitus.

Sometimes Christians object to apologetics on the basis that arguing for a self-existent, eternal being only gets us to a first cause. All we have established thus far is Aristotle's god or the god of the philosophers, not the God of the Bible. The people making the objections claim that the approach is false because we end up with only an incomplete, partial picture of the true God. These people then reject the entire approach to apologetics that we've been discussing in this book.

We must question an underlying assumption here. The key issue is this: Must we have a comprehensive knowledge of God in order to have true knowledge of God? One of the first principles in systematic theology regarding God is the doctrine of His incomprehensibility. This means that no human can now or will ever have a totally exhaustive, comprehensive knowledge and understanding of God. God is infinite in His excellence, and we, even in heaven, will not have an infinite perspective to understand Him. We are finite creatures, and by virtue of our creatureliness, our understanding of God is limited.

If, indeed, a comprehensive picture of God were required to have a true understanding of Him, this would mean that we could have *no* true knowledge of God because we certainly don't have a comprehensive knowledge of Him. Therefore, the fact that our knowledge of God is partial does not mean that our knowledge is untrue.

Even though what we've achieved so far in our reasoning process is only to get to a self-existent, eternal being, that is certainly part of what the Bible reveals to us about the character of God. Whatever else the Bible reveals about the nature of God, it teaches that He is eternal, self-existent, and the One who is the Creator of all things. To that, Aristotle would say, "Yea and amen." Is Aristotle wrong? No. And the fact that a pagan philosopher agrees that there has to be a self-existent, eternal being does not argue against the truth of the Christian claim. In fact, it supports it.

We are simply saying that we agree with Aristotle in the sense that there must be a first cause who is self-existent, pure being, and eternal. It is only a partial point in our knowledge of God, but it is a crucial one. In fact, it is precisely this aspect of the Christian understanding of God that is constantly under attack by atheistic systems of thought.

Atheists attack Christianity at the point of creation and the notion of a transcendent, self-existent, eternal being. So, there is great value in establishing that not only faith but also reason demonstrates the logical necessity of a self-existent, eternal being. Then, the battlefield of the doctrine of God is one where the Christian can emerge victorious rather than surrendering so many of his truth claims.

But again, the question is, How do we get from this self-existent, eternal something to a personal God? That requires a more complex and difficult investigation. One of the most famous arguments for the existence of God is the teleological argument. It is so named because it comes from the Greek word *telos*, which means "end, purpose, goal." Sometimes, it's referred to as the argument from design.

Two of the greatest skeptics in history with respect to

the traditional arguments for God were Immanuel Kant and David Hume. Yet both men felt that the strongest argument from history for the existence of God is found in the teleological argument. Kant said that he could not get past two things: the starry skies above and the moral law within. He was not just a philosopher but also a scientist. He was overwhelmed by the manifest evidence of the presence of design in the world of nature. It is very difficult to attribute design to nature without raising the question of a designer. Can design occur unintentionally? That was the question.

The parable of the invisible gardener, popularized by Antony Flew, tells of explorers in the jungle going through uncharted territory, cutting their way with machetes through a thick rainforest. In the middle of the jungle, they reached a beautifully manicured garden—rows and rows, carefully tilled, everything laid out in perfect symmetry, not a weed among the plants growing there. They reasoned that there must be a gardener, so they searched for him. Unable to find a gardener, they began to speculate whether he was invisible and immaterial. Finally, at the end of the parable, Flew says that God has died the death of a thousand qualifications when we start defining Him as invisible and immaterial. He concludes by asking, "So what is the difference between that God and no God at all?" And the obvious answer is, the garden. Flew still hadn't accounted for the obvious appearance of design in the garden.

This is what the Enlightenment philosophers couldn't get away from. They went from Christian theism to deism (belief in a God who created the world but who is longer active in it) because they couldn't avoid the implications of design. They said the world operates like a perfectly constructed clock with its gears and internal mechanisms, but no one would find a clock without assuming that the clock had a designer or a maker.

Aristotle said that the single most important characteristic of personality is intention, or what was later called—in the nineteenth-century philosophy personalism—"intentionality." For something to act with intention requires a mind and the faculty of choosing what the mind plans. Aristotle said that personality requires intention, intention implies personality, and the essence of intention is found in mind and will.

Impersonal forces have no mind and no will, and they cannot design anything. People only try to reduce God to the level of an impersonal, unintelligent, and nonvolitional force to escape the idea of judgment from One who is intelligent and who does operate by design. That is man's attempt to construct an escape clause from moral indictment. But we cannot have purpose accidentally, and we cannot have intelligence unintelligently. Impersonality cannot produce personality because that would be unintentional intention, and we cannot have intention unintentionally. Just like the concept of self-creation, unintentional intentionality is an absurdity.

If there is design in the universe, then this self-existent, eternal something that is responsible for generating the universe as we find it must be a self-existent, eternal, intelligent being, not merely a something. And if it is intelligent, then it must be personal. And if it is personal, we have now moved away from abstractions and have landed squarely on the pages of sacred Scripture.

Chapter Nine

Kant's Moral Argument

In his watershed work *The Critique of Pure Reason*, Immanuel Kant offered a critique of the traditional arguments for the existence of God. He believed in God, but he did not think that the existence of God could be proven. In this book, Kant gave his famous moral argument for the existence of God. In another of his books, *The Critique of Practical Reason,* he addressed the question of God from a practical standpoint rather than a theological one. In a sense, Kant impolitely ushered God out the front door of the house and then ran around to the kitchen and let Him in the back door.

Before examining Kant's own argument, let's consider what the New Testament teaches in regard to the moral argument for the existence of God. The Apostle Paul says this in Romans: "And since they did not see fit to acknowledge God, God gave them up to a debased mind to do what ought not to be done. They were filled with all manner of unrighteousness, evil, covetousness, malice. They are full of envy, murder, strife, deceit, maliciousness. They are gossips, slanderers, haters of God, insolent, haughty, boastful, inventors of evil, disobedient to parents, foolish, faithless, heartless, ruthless" (1:28–31).

While he doesn't provide an exhaustive list, Paul catalogs the ways in which human beings violate each other with immoral behavior. Then in verse 32, he says, "Though they know God's righteous decree that those who practice such things deserve to die, they not only do them but give approval to those who practice them." Here the Apostle clearly says that God has revealed His holy character to all creatures. All human beings know that God is righteous and have a basic understanding of what that righteousness demands from them with respect to their behavior.

In other words, Paul is saying that every one of us knows the difference between right and wrong. We know how we should behave sexually. We know that we should not rob or murder. We know that it is wrong to be malicious, covetous, or unloving or to engage in the other vices that are listed here in Romans. We know that these things are evil and wrong. Yet despite this clear understanding, we not only engage in these sinful behaviors—knowing that these things are worthy of God's judgment—but we enlist the support of others and encourage them to participate in these sins as well. Pick any sin, and you can find a group of people who militantly argue for that sin's acceptance and toleration in society.

In Romans 2, Paul goes on to say, "For all who have sinned without the law will also perish without the law, and all who have sinned under the law will be judged by the law. . . . For when Gentiles, who do not have the law, by nature do what the law requires, they are a law to themselves, even though they do not have the law" (vv. 12, 14–15). According to this passage, not only did God give the law to Israel in the Ten Commandments, He writes His law on the heart of every creature.

The proof that the law is written on the hearts of men is

the apparatus that we call the conscience. The conscience is part of the constituent makeup of every human being. It is true that consciences can be corrupted, seared, and calloused. If someone is completely devoid of conscience, we call him a psychopath or a sociopath—such a person can commit pernicious wickedness without feeling any sense of guilt whatsoever. This is a perversion of natural humanity.

The Apostle says in Romans 1–2 that God bears witness to Himself by planting His moral law in the heart of every human being. However, the atheist would argue that the human conscience is merely the result of the taboos of the society in which we live. Sigmund Freud argued that these taboos are culturally inflicted, and that the real, free expression of our humanity comes out in unrestrained sexual behavior.

But everyone knows better than that. The conscience simply will not go away. We can argue that in various societies, different things are elevated as law and taboo. For example, some cultures have a taboo against drinking alcohol; other cultures drink alcohol without guilt. Such differences do exist. But every single culture in the world has some sense of an ethical structure, because an ethical structure is necessary for social interaction and the preservation of society. Even in a society plagued by relativism, the conscience cannot be extinguished altogether. This is where Kant's practical and moral arguments come into play.

Kant held it to be a universal phenomenon that every single person in the world has a sense of "oughtness"—what we would call an internal, inherent sense of right and wrong. This sense of oughtness Kant called "the categorical imperative." The categorical imperative represents an absolute command. Kant argued that everyone in the world has a sense of duty that requires and obligates him to behave in a certain manner. We can do everything we can to erase it, deny it, or flee from it, but we cannot get rid of it.

The biggest problem human beings have that they cannot solve is guilt. When discussing religion, theology, or apologetics with atheists, I've often asked them this question: What do you do with your guilt? No one has ever looked me in the eye and responded, "I don't have any guilt." They know that would be untrue. Suddenly, the entire tenor of the discussion moves to a different plane because everyone understands that they have a problem with unresolved guilt.

Kant argued that guilt comes from failing to do what

we are morally obligated to do. He then proceeded in a manner that he defined as *transcendental*. He started with questions of practical necessity rather than pure practicality. When he came to the question of knowledge, he didn't say, "Here's how knowledge takes place." He didn't start by saying that knowledge is possible. Rather, he started with these questions: If knowledge is possible, what would have to be? What are its necessary ingredients? He then constructed his philosophy using that approach.

Kant wanted to know what would be necessary to have true ethics and morality that would impose obligations on humanity. He understood that without some objective standard of behavior, civilization is impossible. Law by sheer preference is simply "might makes right," and we end up with the law of the jungle, which inevitably destroys civilization.

Fyodor Dostoevsky said if there is no God, if there is no ultimate ground for rightness, then all things are permissible. If there's no objective ground for what is right, then everything is simply a battle over preferences—my preference versus yours. Everyone does what is right in his own eyes, and that creates conflict and warfare between groups and between individuals.

Kant was acutely aware of this, and he realized that what was at stake was nothing less than Western civilization. And so, he asked, What is necessary for the categorical imperative—the innate sense of oughtness—to be meaningful? His said the first thing that is required for any ethic to be meaningful is justice, because if crime pays, then there's no practical reason to be virtuous. In fact, there's no practical reason to be anything but selfish. So first, there must be justice, whereby right behavior is rewarded and bad behavior is punished.

The question that followed was, What would be necessary for justice to exist? This is an important question, because we can see that this world does not dispense justice perfectly. Innocent people perish at the hands of the guilty and guilty people go unpunished.

Kant said the first thing that is necessary for justice to exist is life after death. We have to survive the grave to make sure that perfect justice is served. But even if we survive, perhaps the next environment has all of the weaknesses that we have now. So the second thing that is necessary is a judge who is morally perfect. If the judge is not perfectly righteous, then he might administer injustice because he is corrupt, selfish, or liable to bribery. Perfect justice requires perfect judgment, and perfect judgment requires a perfect judge who is above reproach and beyond corruption.

Suppose that such a perfect judge exists. He is morally upright and does the best he can to carry out justice, but unfortunately, there is a limit to his knowledge. Given these limitations, he makes mistakes, because he doesn't know all of the facts or the extenuating circumstances in the cases that come before him. He errs, not out of a corrupt motive, but simply because he is limited in his knowledge. Therefore, if we are to have perfect justice, not only must the judge be morally perfect, but he must also be omniscient. He must know all of the facts so that the judgment he renders is without error and without blemish.

Suppose that all of these are present: life after death, a final judgment, and a judge who is perfectly righteous and who knows everything. Will that now ensure justice? Not yet. One more element must be present to ensure that justice prevails: the judge who is perfect in knowledge, motives, and virtue must also possess the power to enforce his judgments. If he is powerless or restricted in any way in his attempts to bring justice to bear, then there is no guarantee that justice would take place. So this judge must also be omnipotent, stronger than any other force that could possibly hinder his judgments from being carried out.

Kant argued that if the sense of oughtness, the categorical imperative, truly matters, then there is something beyond our earthly lives. And that means that every single person will be held accountable for every single thing he does in life—every evil word, every evil deed, every evil thought, and even every virtuous deed left undone. All will be held accountable by a judge who has no blindfold around his eyes and who is not liable to bribery or corruption, but one who himself is altogether holy, good, and righteous. He knows all, and he is strong enough to bring his judgement to bear.

Kant demolished the traditional arguments for the existence of God but then reconstructed the Judeo-Christian God on the basis of moral arguments. He argued that if morality truly exists, then affirming God is a practical necessity. Kant's ultimate conclusion was that we must live as if there is a God, because if there isn't, we have no hope for civilization and human community.

Chapter Ten

Vanity of Vanities

Immanuel Kant constructed a practical argument for the existence of God from his awareness of what he called the categorical imperative—the sense of morality that is present in every human being. While he did not believe that it is possible to prove the existence of God through normal avenues of research and investigation, he argued that for practical purposes, we must assume that there is a God in order to make life meaningful and society possible.

But not everyone in the philosophical realm agreed

with Kant's conclusion. Cynics and skeptics countered that people cannot believe in God simply because the alternatives are grim. We don't just close our eyes, take a deep breath, and wish with all our might that life is meaningful and that a higher being will ensure that justice is served. Such wishful thinking, they argued, is no grounds for faith.

In the history of philosophy and theoretical thought, the systems related to the arguments for and against the existence of God tend to range between two polar extremes. On one side is full-bodied theism, and on the other side is nihilism. Nihilism comes from the Latin word *nihil,* which means "nothing" or "nothingness." It is not simply the belief that there is no God; nihilism goes further to say that there is no meaning, significance, or sense to human existence. All other philosophies find themselves situated somewhere along this continuum between these two poles.

The Wisdom Literature of the Old Testament wrestles with these two antithetical positions as well, primarily in the book of Ecclesiastes, where two different perspectives are explored. There is life as experienced under the sun and life as experienced under heaven. These may be compared to Kant's distinction between the noumenal world (the realm of God and ideas) and the phenomenal world (the realm where we observe things in the scientific exploration of our senses). He saw a wall between the world that we observe and the transcendent world. This distinction leads to a conflict in the thinking of the Preacher of Ecclesiastes, and it is this: if life only occurs under the sun (the phenomenal realm) and there is no God and life under heaven (the noumenal realm), then the only conclusion to be drawn is "Vanity of vanities! All is vanity" (Eccl. 1:2).

The expression "vanity of vanities" is an expression of the superlative. When Christ is exalted by the New Testament Scriptures, He is called King of kings and Lord of lords. This is a Hebraic way of saying "the supreme King, the supreme Lord." This same idea is encapsulated in the phrase "vanity of vanities." It's an extreme position to conclude that everything is vanity.

What is meant here by the term "vanity" is not the pride of someone who is narcissistic. Here, it is a synonym for futility. What the Preacher is saying, from the vantage point of the phenomenal, is that if there is no God, then everything we do, and everything we encounter in this life, is utterly futile. We are locked in a vicious cycle that has no beginning, no purpose, no significance, and no end. The sun rises. The sun sets. It goes nowhere. This basic underlying philosophy of nihilism is exemplified in Shake-speare's *Macbeth*: "Life's but a walking shadow, a poor player that struts and frets his hour upon the stage and then is heard no more. It is a tale told by an idiot, full of sound and fury, signifying nothing."

Few philosophers are willing to go to that extreme. Most who have rejected full-bodied theism have sought to develop a worldview or philosophical system that exists somewhere between these two poles. But wherever people land on this continuum, they are borrowing capital from one side or the other. Humanism, for example, is extremely naive upon close inspection. Humanists say that there is no God, that our origins come accidentally from a meaning-less event, and that our lives are moving inexorably toward annihilation. They believe that we are meaningless at our origin and meaningless at our destiny, yet at the same time, they fight for human rights and human dignity in between. Humanists simply rest on sentiment and don't have the courage to go where their atheism should naturally drive them—to full nihilism.

That is simply one example of how the philosophical systems in between the two poles borrow capital. There's no basis for believing in human dignity if we're cosmic accidents, but humanists fight for human dignity. They try to sneak in that which they borrow from Judeo-Christianity, even though they categorically reject the source of human dignity.

Writing to the Corinthians, the Apostle Paul put it this way: "And if Christ has not been raised, your faith is futile and you are still in your sins. Then those also who have fallen asleep in Christ have perished. If in Christ we have hope in this life only, we are of all people most to be pitied" (1 Cor. 15:17–19). In other words, unbelievers who do not believe in a resurrection to eternal life should not be angry and hostile toward believers. If anything, they should feel sorry for us as believers because we are missing out on all the pleasures of life. We naively trust God when Christ is nothing but a dead man, and anyone who devotes his life to a dead man is only to be pitied. If there is no basis for confidence in God, then there is no foundation for hope whatsoever, and the inevitable result can only be hopelessness.

Kant, however, did not want to end at hopelessness. He believed that the whole fiber of our humanity, every bone in our bodies, screams to us from our first conscious moment that our lives do have meaning. The labor we undertake—the sweat, blood, and tears that pour out from our passion—has meaning. If we thought that it didn't, we would want to end that labor and end our misery, which is precisely the direction in which that philosophy has gone.

The twentieth-century existential philosopher Albert Camus came to this conclusion: the only serious question left for philosophers to explore is the question of suicide. In other words, Camus said that when people awaken to the reality that there is no God and there are no absolutes, then they grasp that there is no ultimate meaning. People might like the idea of this for a season, for it gives them a vacation from the God of the Bible who says that He will hold them accountable for everything they do. When people conclude that He doesn't exist, they rejoice that they are free to live however they want. This seems wonderful—until they see the cost. And that is what Camus was saying. If humans are not ultimately accountable, then ultimately, we don't count, and life doesn't count. And when we think about the implications of that philosophy, we see why Camus says that the only serious question left is whether we should commit suicide.

Jean-Paul Sartre, in his book *Nausea*, defined man as a useless passion. The title of the book expressed his final comment about the human condition. Sartre noted that human beings are not automatons or robots. We are living, breathing, thinking, choosing human beings. Human life is marked by care and passion. But what if all of these passions and everything we care about are worthless? What if everything we love is meaningless? Then our passions are futile. That was Sartre's conclusion: we are useless passions, and all our cares come to nothing.

This is what Friedrich Nietzsche was driving at when he embraced the concept of nihilism. What the atheistic existential philosophers echoed was this: if we can't know that God exists, it's not enough to build our faith by crossing our fingers and hoping that someone is home up there. If the evidence is to the contrary, if it's true that life has emerged randomly out of the slime, then we must have the moral and intellectual courage to face the grim finality of the results and stare them in the face. We must acknowledge that we came from slime and will return to slime. We are nothing but grown-up germs sitting on one cog of one wheel of a vast cosmic machine that is running down and is destined to annihilation. If that is the truth, we must face reality, and we must not run to religion as an escape from reality.

The driving passion in contemporary culture is escapism through hedonism, and the whole philosophy of hedonism is that we find meaning through pleasure. Maximize pleasure; minimize pain. It's an escape from the pain of having to consider what popular music, the film industry, and the high priests of science are telling us: that we are beasts in human clothing with no ultimate significance. People try to drown out this message with the sound of their music, drugs, or other means of escape. Nietzsche and the skeptics would say that these are not the only drugs. The supreme drug to escape nihilism, according to nineteenth-century atheism, is religion.

Few Christians haven't at some point heard someone say to them, "Your faith is nothing but a crutch that helps you to function and remain mobile when you are, in fact, crippled." That is what a crutch is used for, and the charge is that we use religion as a psychological crutch because we can't bear the message that we're getting from all sides. And so, we turn to religion as the ultimate form of escape, the ultimate drug, the ultimate crutch—what Karl Marx referred to as the opiate of the masses, a narcotic to dull our senses to minimize pain. In other words, religious people are just one brand of hedonists who seek their pleasure in escaping from the real world of futile passions, futile labor, and death.

The nineteenth-century atheists did not endeavor to disprove the existence of God. Rather, their opening assumption was that there is no God. The biggest problem they had was attempting to answer this question: Since there is no God, why is it that human beings are incurably religious? Why is it that man can be defined not only as *homo sapiens* but as *homo religiosis*—man, the religious person? Wherever we go throughout the world, we find that the vast majority of people engage in some kind of religious activity. From a Christian standpoint, that religion may be complete idolatry, but nevertheless, it is still religion.

The most common answer that these thinkers gave was that religion is caused by psychological fear. In other words, the main reason that people believe in God is that they're afraid of the consequences if there is no God. Ludwig Feuerbach said that the main reason we create God in our own image is because we understand that without God, we are doomed. Without God, we are in a hopeless situation. We are indeed a useless passion, and we can't bear the grimness of nihilism. So to escape nihilism, we leapfrog over all of these intermediate options and affirm the existence of God as a narcotic to dull our senses and pain. Therefore, the number one argument against theism in the nineteenth century was that theism is simply the result of the psychological needs of naive people.

But are these nihilistic, atheistic thinkers correct? Upon further examination, the truth is that the shoe may actually be on the other foot. Or in this case, we might say that the crutch may in fact be for the other leg.

Chapter Eleven

The Psychology of Atheism

The nineteenth-century atheists argued that religion results from the creative imaginations of human beings who simply lack the moral courage to face the cold, stark reality of the ultimate meaninglessness of human life. In other words, a psychological need to escape grim reality drives people to formulate for themselves the idea of a God who they hope will rescue them from meaninglessness. This was their answer to the question, If there is no God, why are there theists? Yet the question could be turned around on these skeptics: If there is a God, why are there people who deny His existence?

How could some of the most brilliant thinkers in history come to such different conclusions about the existence of God? Though I radically disagree with Jean-Paul Sartre in his understanding of reality, he was certainly one of the most insightful, engaging, acute thinkers of the modern era. John Stuart Mill was also a giant in terms of intellectual power, as were Immanuel Kant, David Hume, Ludwig Feuerbach, Friedrich Nietzsche, and others.

Yet on the other side of the argument, we have great thinkers such as Thomas Aquinas, Augustine of Hippo, Anselm of Canterbury, and other titans who have defended the theistic arguments. So clearly, this is not simply a question of superior intellect. One of the factors that absolutely must be included in this debate is the psychological factor. We must agree from the start that the question of the existence of God is loaded with psychological baggage.

The reality of God cannot be determined on the basis of what people want to be true. Kant's critics are correct in that regard: just because life would be meaningless without God does not provide sufficient grounds to argue for His existence. The meaninglessness of life without God reveals the state of our subjectivity and our desires, but it doesn't prove the existence of God.

However, it must also be acknowledged that everyone who gets involved in a discussion on the existence of God has psychological baggage, even those who argue against His existence. Those who deny the existence of God have an enormous vested interest in denying Him because He stands as the greatest obstacle in the universe to their own autonomy. If we want to live with impunity, our highest obstacle is a self-existent, eternal God who is righteous and just. For unrepentant sinners, the worst thing that could befall them is to fall into the hands of the living God. As a result, denying God is absolutely necessary for living with impunity. People will do anything in their power to deny their guilt and culpability, even to the point of denying that they are accountable for their existence.

A psychology for God doesn't prove His existence any more than a psychology against God disproves His existence. Arguments for the existence of God must be established on an objective basis, not on the basis of subjective preference. But the charge against Christians that they believe in God only out of psychological wish fulfillment is not a one-way accusation. There is just as much psychological desire for the atheist to deny the existence of God as there is for the theist who wants to affirm the existence of God.

The Bible speaks directly and clearly to this very issue. Scripture teaches that fallen man, in his sinfulness, will not have God in his thinking. Our natural, mortal condition involves having reprobate minds that have been darkened—so darkened by prejudice that we do not want to even open the window a crack to allow the rays of God's self-revelation into our heads. We know what's at stake, and we know that we are in trouble if we allow that knowledge in.

The Apostle Paul develops this idea in his letter to the church at Rome. In Romans 1, he argues that the invisible things of God can be known through the created universe. This statement contradicts the skepticism and agnosticism of Immanuel Kant because Paul says that not only can we know God through nature, but in fact, we do know God through nature.

Paul rejects the idea that those who are not theists choose this path because they have an intellectual problem with the existence of God or because they have insufficient information or because God's manifestation of Himself has been obscured. Their problem is not intellectual but moral. It is not that they can't know God but that they don't want God. That is Paul's conclusion, and as a result, he says, "The wrath of God is revealed from heaven against all ungodliness and unrighteousness of men, who by their unrighteousness suppress the truth" (Rom. 1:18).

That sentence draws a reaction in many people. The last thing they want to believe in is a God of wrath. Many theists who affirm the existence of God deny that the God they affirm is capable of wrath. But the word Paul uses is a strong one. It denotes a violent eruption of passion. Paul is saying that not only is God angry, He is furious.

In this text, God is not angry with righteous or innocent people. His wrath is revealed from heaven against unrighteousness and ungodliness. This is a grammatical construction called a *hendiadys*, where two different words are used to describe the same thing. The Apostle is saying that there is one particular sin that has caused God's anger to boil over, and that particular sin could be described both as unrighteousness and ungodliness. What is the sin in view here? Suppressing the truth in unrighteousness. It is an evil repression of truth that Paul is describing.

God is angry because He has given humankind

knowledge that is not vague or obscure. God has manifested Himself clearly to every human being. Paul's radical affirmation is that every single person knows that God exists because God has shown Himself in a clear demonstration through the things He has made. But humans by nature hold down this knowledge and try to bury it.

Later on in this text, the Apostle Paul says, "They exchanged the truth about God for a lie and worshiped and served the creature rather than the Creator, who is blessed forever! Amen" (Rom. 1:25). Paul makes this activity of the human mind the primary, foundational act of evil committed by fallen human beings: the idolatry of exchanging the truth and trading it to embrace a lie.

The Apostle is saying that there is a psychology to atheism. What we fear more than nature, more than meaninglessness, is that we will be held accountable by a God who is holy, because in the presence of the holy, we are immediately exposed as unholy. The God of Scripture is a God who is omniscient and knows everything about us. He is a God who is omnipotent, all-powerful. He is a God who is altogether holy.

And worst of all, He is a God who is immutable. There is no hope that He will ever grow weak and lose

His omnipotence. There is no hope that He will ever lose His knowledge of everything that we've ever done. There is no hope that He will ever compromise His righteousness or holiness, because He is immutably holy, immutably omnipotent, and immutably omniscient.

All of these things are revealed through nature, and we know them by nature. And because that is so terrifying, it is our basic disposition as fallen creatures to have a vested interest in fleeing, just as Adam and Eve fled the garden and hid in the bushes because they were naked and ashamed. That is the biggest barrier that humans beings have when coming to a full understanding of God. The question of the existence of God is not a question confined to the intellectual realm. The real reason that anyone denies the existence of God is simply this: that we too are naked, and we know it.

About the Author

Dr. R.C. Sproul was founder of Ligonier Ministries, founding pastor of Saint Andrew's Chapel in Sanford, Fla., first president of Reformation Bible College, and executive editor of *Tabletalk* magazine. His radio program, *Renewing Your Mind*, is still broadcast daily on hundreds of radio stations around the world and can also be heard online. He was author of more than one hundred books, including *The Holiness of God*, *Chosen by God*, and *Everyone's a Theologian*. He was recognized throughout the world for his articulate defense of the inerrancy of Scripture and the need for God's people to stand with conviction upon His Word.

Get 3 free months
of *Tabletalk*

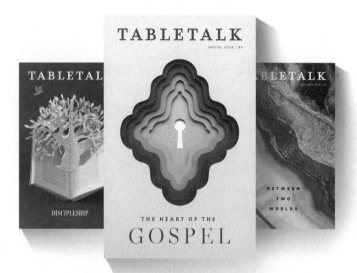

In 1977, R.C. Sproul started *Tabletalk* magazine.
Today it has become the most widely read subscriber-based monthly
devotional magazine in the world. **Try it free for 3 months.**

𝕋 TryTabletalk.com/CQ | 800.435.4343